FLORAL ESTRANGEMENTS

FLORAL ESTRANGEMENTS

Taunt Your Rivals & Vanquish Your Enemies through the Language of Flowers

BY REBECCA FISHBEIN

CHRONICLE BOOKS
SAN FRANCISCO

Library of Congress Cataloging-in-Publication Data

Names: Fishbein, Rebecca, author.
Title: Floral estrangements : taunt your rivals and vanquish your enemies
    through the language of flowers / by Rebecca Fishbein.
Description: San Francisco : Chronicle Books, [2024]
Identifiers: LCCN 2024017830 | ISBN 9781797231020 (hardcover)
Subjects: LCSH: Flower language.
Classification: LCC GR780 .F57 2024 | DDC 745.92--dc23/eng/20240515
LC record available at https://lccn.loc.gov/2024017830

Manufactured in China.

Illustrations by Jill De Haan.
Design by Evelyn Furuta.

10 9 8 7 6 5 4 3 2 1

Chronicle books and gifts are available at special quantity discounts to
corporations, professional associations, literacy programs, and other
organizations. For details and discount information, please contact
our premiums department at corporatesales@chroniclebooks.com or at
1-800-759-0190.

Chronicle Books LLC
680 Second Street
San Francisco, California 94107
www.chroniclebooks.com

CONTENTS

CONTENTS

GLOSSARY

Amaryllis
Pride

Anemone
Forsaken

Azalea
Fragile love

Basil
Hatred

Begonia
Beware

Bird's-foot Trefoil
My revenge

Black-eyed Susan
Justice

Buttercup
Immaturity

Candytuft
Indifference

Carnation
PURPLE
Capriciousness

Carnation
TWO-TONED
Parting/no

Carnation
YELLOW
Disappointment/rejection

Chrysanthemum
YELLOW
Slighted love

Columbine
Foolishness

Cyclamen
Resignation/goodbye

Daffodil
Unrequited love

Delphinium
PURPLE
Haughtiness

Dill
Lust

Evening Primrose
Fickleness/inconsistency

Geranium
Stupidity/folly

Gladiolus
Give me a break

Grass
Submission

Hellebore
Scandal

Hollyhock
Ambition

Hyacinth
PURPLE
Sorrow/regret

Hyacinth
YELLOW
Jealousy

Hydrangea
Frigidity/heartlessness

Larkspur
PINK
Fickleness

Lily
ORANGE
Hatred

Lily
YELLOW
Falseness

Marigold
Cruelty/grief/jealousy

Mock Orange
Deceit

Monkshood
Beware / a deadly foe is near

Nasturtium
Conquest / victory in battle

Oleander
Caution/beware

Peony
Shame

Petunia
Resentment/anger

Pine
Pity

Poet's Narcissus
Egotism

Poppy
Eternal sleep / oblivion

Rhododendron
Danger

Rose
BLACK
Hatred

Rose
DARK CRIMSON
Mourning

Rose
DRIED WHITE
Death is preferable to loss of virtue

Rose
WITHERED WHITE
You made no impression

Rose
YELLOW
Infidelity

Snapdragon
Deception

Sunflower
False riches

Tansy
Hostile thoughts / I declare war on you

Willow
Sadness/mourning

INTRODUCTION

The act of gifting flowers is a curious ritual: "Here, I love you, watch something die." And yet, flowers have always been used to send messages. Loved ones give each other flowers for all sorts of life events, like graduations, weddings, funerals, anniversaries, and forgotten anniversaries.

The Victorians took flowers even more seriously. They believed that every flower had a symbolic meaning—good, bad, and everything in between. Give someone a honeysuckle and you pledge your devotion. A pansy lets the giftee know you're thinking about them. A rose says I love you . . . *most of the time.*

In this book, you'll find the bad flowers. These flowers seek revenge.

They demand justice.

They take no shit.

They let flaky friends know you're tired of being ditched.

They make bad bosses stop calling you on your days off.

They tell cheaters they better beware.

Sift through our detailed floriography featuring fifty vengeful flowers, ranging from the merely miffed to the truly hate-filled. You'll also find twenty original bouquet recipes for your worst enemies and closest frenemies, cruel lovers and ex-lovers, capricious colleagues, messy roommates, and even one for your health insurance company, for obvious reasons. Thanks to this book, next time someone wrongs you, they'll get what they deserve: a tasteful arrangement, with a dash of spite.

Amaryllis

Pride

Family: Amaryllidaceae | **Genus:** *Amaryllis*
Common names: belladonna lily, naked lady

Amaryllis plants are known for their pink-and-white funnel-shaped flowers, which sit atop a long, upright leafless stem. They somewhat resemble lilies, hence their nicknames, though the two plants are not actually related. Amaryllis are typically native to South Africa, but you can also find plants in Australia and on the West Coast in the United States, as they thrive in coastal areas.

The ancient Greeks believed that Amaryllis was a nymph who fell in love with a shepherd named Alteo. Every day, to demonstrate her love for him, she would pierce herself in the heart with a golden arrow. Alteo wasn't feeling it, though, and eventually the blood from all the heart-piercing consumed her and transformed her into a red amaryllis. That myth, in tandem with the amaryllis's ramrod-straight stem and refusal to succumb to the harshest of weather conditions, has given it the symbolic meaning of pride, like the kind you throw away when you triple-text your crush before posting a thirst trap to your Instagram story after spotting them online.

Anemone

Forsaken

Family: Ranunculaceae | **Genus:** *Anemone*
Common names: anemone, windflower

The anemone is a flowering plant in the buttercup family Ranunculaceae, recognizable by its upright stems and vibrant colors. The anemone signifies "forsaken," making it the perfect flower to send the man you went on one great date with before he unmatched you on Hinge without explanation. According to Greek myth, the anemone flower is partially made from the blood of the hunter Adonis, who was gored to death by a wild boar, so perhaps you'll get lucky and the same fate will befall Hinge man.

Azalea

Fragile love

Family: Ericaceae | **Genus:** *Rhododendron*
Common name: azalea

Azaleas are loosely branched flowering shrubs often characterized by their effusive pink, red, white, or yellow petals, sweet
fragrance, and preference for partial shade. Native to several
continents, including Europe and North America in the Northern
Hemisphere, azaleas prefer to bloom in the early spring and love a nice
rain shower. While beautiful, azalea petals easily fall from the stem, hence
their association with fragile love, the kind that can shatter with one
fight, one misinterpreted text, or one ill-timed fart in a sexy moment.

An azalea can be gifted to anyone with whom your developing romance
is mere seconds from dissolving—the not-so-great text returner, the
first date you showed up thirty minutes late for, the person you tricked
into making out with you by pretending you were obsessed with their
favorite band, the hot dentist you are convinced was flirting with you
when she complimented your healthy gums, etc.

Basil

---○---

Hatred

Family: Lamiaceae | **Genus:** *Ocimum*
Common name: common basil

Basil is a culinary herb native to tropical regions and used in a wide variety of cuisines. The schools of thought are split on where basil got its name. Some think it comes from the Greek *basileus,* meaning "royal," because the sweet-smelling and tasty herb was fit for royalty. Others think the name is derived from the mythical basilisk, a monstrous serpent who could kill you just by looking at you—allegedly, the ancient Greeks believed basil looked like a basilisk's deadly jaws. The latter definition has given basil a long-lasting association with hatred, and though most of us are not yet blessed with the power to murder someone with one stare, handing a sprig or two of basil to the upstairs neighbor who just took up tap dancing should still send the right message.

Begonia

Beware

Family: Begoniaceae | **Genus:** *Begonia*
Common names: none

This tropical evergreen plant is praised for its ostentatious foliage, but it's also a symbol of warning, making it an excellent present for the officemate whose incessant gum-chewing—and I mean ALL. DAY. LONG.—is wearing you down to your last nerve. ASHLEY, I SWEAR TO GOD, I HOPE YOUR TEETH FALL OUT.

You can also consider gifting a red begonia to any Grateful Dead enthusiast who makes or even suggests you listen to a twelve-hour concert album. They'll think it's a nice homage to Jerry Garcia, but you know the truth.

Bird's-foot Trefoil

---◦---

My revenge

Family: Fabaceae | **Genus:** *Lotus*
Common names: common bird's-foot trefoil, eggs and bacon,
butter and eggs, granny's toenails

Bird's-foot trefoil is a perennial herbaceous plant native to European and Asian grasslands, though you can also find it in the United Kingdom and the United States. It gets its creative name from the pillowy shape of its leaves, which resemble small slippers. (Another interpretation: creepy nails, hence the nickname "granny's toenails.") To the Victorians, bird's-foot trefoil symbolized revenge, and handing someone a bird's-foot bouquet served as a warning that things were about to get karmically *real*. These flowers make an excellent gift for all your favorite people: the former college bestie who made out with the guy you brought to your sorority formal, the preschool teacher who said your skill with scissors was below standard, the driver who cut you off this morning. Bird's-foot trefoil for them all.

Black-eyed Susan

Justice

Family: Asteraceae | **Genus:** *Rudbeckia*
Common names: brown-eyed Susan, brown Betty, golden Jerusalem

Black-eyed Susans are upright annual flowering plants native to the US Great Plains, though they are now found growing in all fifty states, as well as in Canada. (Black-eyed Susans are so ubiquitous in the United States, they're even the state flower of Maryland.) Known for their cheerful sunflower-like yellow petals, they get their name from their prominent dark centers—which, to be clear, are brown and not black, though no need to quibble over eye color. Black-eyed Susans have come to symbolize justice, with the golden petals surrounding a dark center eye representing goodness overtaking evil. This makes them the ideal flower to, say, lay across your romantic partner's pillow after they finally admit that your lasagna recipe is superior.

Buttercup

─── ◦ ───

Immaturity

Family: Ranunculaceae | **Genus:** *Ranunculus*
Common names: spearwort, water crowfoot

Buttercups are perennial flowering plants often recognized by their simple, bulbous yellow petals that curve inward, giving them their namesake cup shape. That same inward curve reflects light in a way that makes buttercups appear particularly bright and appealing, though most gardeners would consider them weeds. Buttercups can represent youthful joy—a pre-Netflix children's game involved holding a buttercup under one's chin to create a yellow reflection—but they also symbolize immaturity, which means you should definitely give one to the ex who made it clear they'd rather date their Nintendo Switch than you.

Candytuft

Indifference

Family: Brassicaceae | **Genus:** *Iberis*
Common names: iberis, candytuft

Native to southern Europe, candytuft is a ground-hugging, ever-green flowering plant recognizable for its white (and occasionally pink and purple) blooms that pop up from late spring to early summer. Because candytufts are able to bloom regardless of the weather conditions, they've come to signify "indifference" in the language of flowers. This makes them useful presents for a wide variety of people: the cute friend of a friend you have *not* been trying to flirt with, your competitive sibling, the ex who keeps liking all your Instagram photos, the colleague who signs all their emails "Best" and refuses to include a single exclamation point in their reply, no matter how many you used in your original message. You don't care about any of this at all, not you, no sirree!

Carnation
PURPLE

---•---

Capriciousness

Family: Caryophyllaceae | **Genus:** *Dianthus*
Common name: pinks

Carnations are flowering herbaceous plants native to the Mediterranean, typically beloved for their unique fringed petals and spicy scents. Though carnations have earned the nickname "pinks," due to the fact that they initially only came in one or two shades, years of cultivation have created an array of carnation colors that each have their own symbolic meanings, much like Skittles. Purple carnations symbolize capriciousness—feel free to leave a few on your boss's desk after she makes you rewrite the same report for the fifteenth time because she keeps changing her mind about whether or not to use Oxford commas.

Carnation
TWO-TONED

———◦———

Parting/no

Family: Caryophyllaceae | **Genus:** *Dianthus*
Common name: pinks

Another misnamed member of the "pinks" gang, two-toned, or striped, carnations have come to symbolize parting, or a way of telling someone no. Back in the day, people would use carnations as a response to someone's romantic overture. If you gave your prospective paramour a solid carnation, you were telling them yes, while a striped carnation was a no. There's no need to let this tradition stay in the past—the next time someone creepily slides into your DMs, feel free to hit them with a pic of this fancy little guy.

Carnation
YELLOW

Disappointment/rejection

Family: Caryophyllaceae | **Genus:** *Dianthus*
Common name: pinks

Yellow carnations have come to symbolize disappointment and rejection. As with two-toned carnations, in the olden times, gifting someone a yellow carnation was a way to break up with them, although a somewhat more forceful one. Consider this method a viable alternative to blocking the Tinder date who showed up to drinks two hours late and ordered three twenty-five-dollar cocktails before insisting that you foot the bill—because he's a feminist.

Chrysanthemum
YELLOW

———◦———

Slighted love

Family: Asteraceae | **Genus:** *Chrysanthemum*
Common name: mums

Chrysanthemums are colorful flowering plants native to East Asia and northeastern Europe, although you can now find them in gardens all over the world. There are about forty different species categorized under the chrysanthemum genus, and many of them hold different meanings in the language of flowers. In the Victorian era, for instance, certain chrysanthemums were symbols of sympathy or condolence, and in modern Europe and parts of Asia, they're often used as funeral flowers. But yellow chrysanthemums have a special meaning—slighted love, like the kind you experience when you bring a friend to the coffee shop to scope out your barista crush, and the crush hits on *them* instead. Rude.

Columbine

Foolishness

Family: Ranunculaceae | **Genus:** *Aquilegia*
Common name: granny's bonnet

Native to Europe and North America, columbines are perennial flowering plants known for their unique multicolored petals and hardy natures. Columbines are often found in wooded areas, meadows, and mountain ranges. They have tubular, almost spiky long-spurred flowers that tend to be bicolored in a wide range of hues, including whites, reds, yellows, and blues. Despite their beauty, they've come to symbolize foolishness, probably because their pointy, colorful flowers look like court jesters' hats.

Shakespeare used columbines as a reference to foolishness in *Hamlet*. In early modern Italy, a recurring theater character named Columbina fell in love with the royal court's "fool." This makes columbines great flowers for, say, the spouse who cannot figure out how to turn on the new vacuum, no matter how many YouTube tutorials you text them, or the housemate who insists on bringing home dates who *definitely* have bedbugs.

Cyclamen

―――――◦―――――

Resignation/goodbye

Family: Primulaceae | **Genus:** *Cyclamen*
Common names: sowbread, Persian violet, primrose

These gorgeous perennial flowering plants are native to the Mediterranean and the Middle East, and are characterized by pink, purple, red, or white upswept petals. In many cultures, cyclamen symbolize resignation and goodbye, and gifting someone a potted cyclamen is a suitable way to bid that person farewell. Keep this bloom in mind the next time your boss talks down to you during a department-wide meeting before asking you to teach him how to open a Google Doc.

Daffodil

───────○───────

Unrequited love

Family: Amaryllidaceae | **Genus:** *Narcissus*
Common names: Lent lily, Easter lily, Peter's leek

The national flower of Wales, daffodils are native to northern Europe, though you can find them growing all over the world. They're primarily recognized for their cheerful yellow petals and a single crown-like structure in the center called the "corona," or "trumpet." Daffodils mean quite a few things in the language of flowers—since they tend to bloom in late winter or early spring, they've come to symbolize rebirth and renewal, among other things. But for the purposes of this book, we'll stick with one of their darker meanings: unrequited love.

Daffodils come from the genus *Narcissus*, so they're associated with the Greek myth of the egotistical Narcissus and the nymph Echo. As the story goes, Echo fell in love with Narcissus, but Narcissus was only into his own reflection; in fact, when he spotted his reflection in a pool of water, he fell so deeply in love with it that he ultimately perished while staring at himself, leaving poor Echo totally brokenhearted. Just something to think about the next time you crush on someone who seems more interested in their own thirst traps than in you.

Delphinium
PURPLE

---○---

Haughtiness

Family: Ranunculaceae | **Genus:** *Delphinium*
Common names: purple passion, pagan purples, candle larkspur

Delphiniums are herbaceous plants in the buttercup family, found all over the Northern Hemisphere and in parts of Africa. They're notable for their tall, elegant stalks covered in flowers that come in an array of colors, including blue, pink, and violet. Delphiniums signify a number of things in the language of flowers, including levity, dignity, and the strong bond of love. But purple larkspurs in particular symbolize haughtiness—like the kind emanating from the cool tweens trying on the same crop top and lowriders as you in the department store dressing room.

Dill

Lust

Family: Apiaceae | **Genus:** *Anethum*
Common name: dill weed

Dill is an herb in the parsley family, one native to the Mediterranean region and southeastern Europe. You've probably seen dill in grocery store form, but in nature, dill grows as long stalks of green with branched-out leaves, topped with small yellow flowers. In addition to making every dish taste like a masterpiece, dill also serves as a symbol of lust, probably because sprinkling it on a BLT creates something better than sex. Indeed, its erotic potential made dill a prime ingredient in olden-day love potions, in case you're thinking about making a dill smoothie for the cutie who moved across the hall but still hasn't bothered flirting with you—plus, you can use any extra sauce to dress your next salmon cutlet.

Evening Primrose

Fickleness/inconsistency

Family: Primulaceae | **Genus:** *Primula*
Common name: primrose

Evening primroses are flowering plants that hail from mountainous regions in the Northern Hemisphere, though they're cultivated all over the world for their beautiful, fragrant flowers. There are many species of evening primrose, but typically, they are low-growing plants that bloom in early spring, with bunched flowers that come in yellow, red, pink, blue, purple, or white. Evening primroses have a number of symbolic meanings, including fickleness (i.e., lacking firmness or consistency in devotion), making them a great gift for the crush who waits hours to respond to your text with nothing but an "Lol" yet still wants to hang out on Saturday night.

Geranium

— ◦ —

Stupidity/folly

Family: Geraniaceae | **Genus:** *Geranium*
Common names: cranesbill, hardy geranium, true geranium

Primarily native to southern Africa, geraniums are flowering plants found in garden beds, window boxes, and hanging pots across the United States. They're known for their soft, velvety petals and bright colors. Since they thrive in contained spaces, they're easy to grow, which makes them common indoor and outdoor houseplants for even casual gardeners. Despite their beauty and popularity, in the Victorian era, geraniums symbolized stupidity and folly—you know, in case you want to give yourself a present the next time you accidentally pour an entire pot of boiling pasta water on your own hand. It happens!

Gladiolus

Give me a break

Family: Iridaceae | **Genus:** *Gladiolus*
Common name: sword lily

Gladioli are flowering offshoots of the iris family, native to Europe, Africa, and the Mediterranean. They're particularly notable for their long stems, funnel-shaped flowers, and swordlike leaves— hence the name *gladiolus*, which means "little sword" in Latin. Many myths exist about the gladiolus; some people even believe they're the "lilies of the field" mentioned in Jesus's biblical Sermon on the Mount. There are also many symbolic meanings associated with gladioli, but for the purposes of this floriography, they symbolize "give me a break." You can take this literally and hand a sprig of gladiolus to your boss amid a particularly grueling workday, or skew more side-eye and wave one emphatically at the TV every time a *Bachelor* contestant cries at the camera and says she's in love.

Grass

———◆———

Submission

Family: Poaceae | **Genus:** *Poa*
Common name: I mean, it's grass.

You are likely familiar with grass, a low, green plant found nearly all over the world. There are many different types of grass, but generally the plant manifests as hollow, green stems with blade-like leaves and occasional flowering heads. Grass is essential to our ecosystem, providing nutrition and shelter for animals and insects as well as for humans, when necessary. Despite its ubiquitousness, grass does have the slightly negative symbolic meaning of submission, probably because everybody's always walking all over it. Throw some blades of grass at your colleague who's always sucking up to management, or hand a couple of blades to the friend who totally changed when they started dating some guy and now claims they're "obsessed" with the *Fast & Furious* franchise.

Hellebore

---◦---

Scandal

Family: Ranunculaceae | **Genus:** *Helleborus*
Common names: Christmas rose, winter rose, Lenten rose

A witchy addition to this floriography, hellebores are beautiful—though incredibly lethal!—herbaceous plants in the buttercup family. Native to Eurasia, hellebores tend to bloom in late winter and are characterized by their short stems, thick, clumped leaves, and ostentatious flowers. Though hellebores are not related to the rose family, their showy cupped petals are roselike in nature, lending them nicknames like "Christmas rose" and "winter rose." Since the hellebore is able to bloom in more wintry conditions, it was once believed to have magical powers—though really its magic is more that it'll kill you if you eat it. Among its many other symbolic meanings, the hellebore represents scandal, making it an excellent gift for the friend you are absolutely convinced is cheating on their partner but refuses to come clean, no matter how many strong drinks you buy them in hopes of prying it out of them. It's not like you're going to tell anyone about it. You just want the tea.

Hollyhock

─────◦─────

Ambition

Family: Malvaceae | **Genus:** *Alcea*
Common name: common hollyhock

Hollyhock, or *Alcea rosea*, is an herbaceous flowering plant native
to China, though you can find its handsome flowers all over
the world. They're exceptionally beautiful plants, with supertall,
narrow stems covered with large flowers that tend to come in white,
pink, red, or yellow. Likely thanks to its towering stance, hollyhock
symbolizes ambition—like the kind you lost when you discovered that
no matter how hard you worked to advance in your career, you still
couldn't afford to buy a house. Thanks for nothing, avocado toast habit.

Hyacinth
PURPLE

---•---

Sorrow/regret

Family: Asparagaceae | **Genus:** *Hyacinthus*
Common names: common hyacinth, Dutch hyacinth, garden hyacinth

Native to the Mediterranean and tropical Africa, hyacinths are ornate, spring-blooming plants often characterized by the striking, fragrant flower spikes that cover their stalks. Each color hyacinth offers a different meaning, with purple hyacinths symbolizing sorrow and regret, like the kind you feel when you get to the coffee shop too late on a Sunday and all the chocolate croissants have already sold out. Be sure to bring a sprig or two of purple hyacinth with you to lay atop the pastry display case—it won't bring the croissants back, but it'll send a strong message to the heartless customer who snagged the last one.

Hyacinth
YELLOW

———◦———

Jealousy

Family: Asparagaceae | **Genus:** *Hyacinthus*
Common names: common hyacinth, Dutch hyacinth, garden hyacinth

Hyacinths have a starring role in Greek mythology and are named after Hyacinthus, a young man with whom the god Apollo fell passionately in love. Allegedly, the god Zephyrus was also in love with Hyacinthus and, out of jealousy, blew Apollo's discus off course during a friendly game, beheading Hyacinthus in the process. The irony! Perhaps because of this story, yellow hyacinths have come to signify jealousy, so feel free to hand one to the hot guy in your yoga class who brought his girlfriend the other day. It's probably a better move than beheading him, not that we'd judge you either way.

Hydrangea

———◦———

Frigidity/heartlessness

Family: Hydrangeaceae | **Genus:** *Hydrangea*
Common names: hortensia, sevenbark

Hydrangeas are a genus of flowering shrubs native to the Western Hemisphere and eastern Asia. They're notable for their large, globe-shaped flower clusters that come in an array of colors, including blue, purple, pink, and white. Hydrangeas are associated with a number of meanings in the language of flowers, including frigidity and heartlessness, the latter of which stems from the aforementioned magnificent flower clusters that produce few seeds despite their general abundance. Basically, while these are beautiful flowers, they don't really offer a lot in return, much like your supercute date from last week who spoke in monosyllables and didn't bother asking you a single question.

Larkspur
PINK

———◦———

Fickleness

Family: Ranunculaceae | **Genus:** *Consolida*
Common names: lark's-claw, lark-heel

Larkspurs have different meanings depending on their hue. Pink larkspurs can represent fickleness, making a single pink larkspur the ideal gift for the coworker who asked you to have lunch with them last week, then conveniently "forgot" about the invite and went to Sweetgreen with Calvin from billing instead. Not like you weren't jonesing for a Guacamole Greens yourself or anything.

Lily
ORANGE

— ◦ —

Hatred

Family: Liliaceae | **Genus:** *Lilium*
Common names: hleri, hr̥t, lily

Native to temperate areas in the Northern Hemisphere, lilies are some of the oldest cultivated plants in the world, often used among ancient civilizations as medicine and food as well as for ornamental purposes. They're known for their upright, leafy stems and elegant singular flowers, which often form trumpet or tubelike shapes, though some lilies are bulb- or bowl-shaped instead. Lilies have many meanings in the language of flowers, with different symbolism attributed to different colors.

Orange lilies are probably the darkest of all and signify hatred. Feel free to toss a stem at all your fiercest enemies: your college roommate whose alarm always went off at 6 a.m., the ex-boyfriend who broke up with you over Instagram DM, the boss who bought everyone a birthday gift except for you, the cousin who went to Harvard. Orange lilies for all those monsters.

Lily
YELLOW

———•———

Falseness

Family: Liliaceae | **Genus:** *Lilium*
Common names: hleri, hṛṭ, lily

Yellow lilies represent falseness, making them excellent gifts for all the lying liars in your life. Send a stem by messenger to the date whose Bumble profile said they were thirty-two when they were really forty-six. Leave a sprig on the doorstep of the former college bestie who said she definitely did *not* hook up with your ex while you were studying abroad. Craft a wreath for the downstairs neighbor who says he's not stealing your packages yet seems to own a large number of sweaters you're pretty sure you ordered but never received. Save a few yellow lilies for yourself while you're at it. You know what you did.

Marigold

Cruelty/grief/jealousy

Family: Asteraceae | **Genus:** *Tagetes*
Common names: drunkards, Mary's gold

Marigolds are herbs native to several parts of the Americas, including southwestern North America, South America, and the tropics. Their flowers tend to comprise yellow, red, or orange petals that cluster together in a cup or ball shape, though some varieties are less globular than others. Marigolds are so cheerful and inviting that in Mexico, they are used to celebrate Día de los Muertos, or Day of the Dead, as it's believed that the marigold's bright colors will lead the dead to the land of the living for their annual visit. Yet in the Victorian language of flowers, marigolds have dark symbolic meanings, including cruelty, jealousy, and grief. These flowers are for those jerks who broke your heart, whether they be a cheating ex, a best friend who friend-dumped you, or the pizza shop that sent your pepperoni pie to the wrong address when you were absolutely STARVING.

Mock Orange

Deceit

Family: Hydrangeaceae | **Genus:** *Philadelphus*
Common name: mock orange

*P*hiladelphus is a genus of flowering shrub native to a host of regions, including northern Asia and Japan, Mexico, and parts of the United States. Characterized by its fragrant, showy white blossoms that both look and smell like orange blossoms, philadelphus has earned the nickname "mock orange," though it bears no actual relation to the citrus. It is perhaps because of this deception that mock orange has the symbolic meaning of deceit, similar to how that $1,800 dining table you bought from Instagram was marketed as "real wood" when it was clearly made out of plastic. Lay a mock orange blossom across your now-shattered piece of faux midcentury furniture as a reminder to never again purchase something nonrefundable off an app.

Monkshood

Beware / a deadly foe is near

Family: Ranunculaceae | **Genus:** *Aconitum*
Common names: wolfsbane, aconite, friar's cap

Monkshood is a flowering herb in the buttercup family, native to the north temperate zone. Monkshood plants are characterized by their fingerlike leaves and hood-shaped flowers that tend to come in purple or blue hues, although some color variation exists. Monkshood has served many purposes in different cultures. Its historic uses run the gamut from healing to witchcraft. These plants have a number of symbolic meanings and are often used to warn of danger or a nearby foe. This makes it a great plant to tape up next to the gaping hole behind your oven so you can alert the mouse family living there that your cat is onto them.

FLORAL ESTRANGEMENTS

Nasturtium

Conquest / victory in battle

Family: Tropaeolaceae | **Genus:** *Tropaeolum*
Common name: Indian cress

Nasturtiums are annual and perennial flowering plants native to South and Central America, though they've also invaded several other continents. They're known for their bright, picturesque funnel-shaped flowers—which come in vivid yellows, reds, and oranges—as well as their smooth and circular leaves. The leaves and flowers are both edible and have a peppery taste, making them excellent garnishes for dishes calling for a pop of color and touch of heat.

Nasturtiums symbolize conquest and victory in battle: Give one to the cute new neighbor who smiles at you for the first time, hand a sprig to your teacher when he *finally* praises your work, or sprinkle some in your mom's salad when she admits that she was wrong about your second-grade haircut.

Oleander

———•———

Caution/beware

Family: Apocynaceae | **Genus:** *Nerium*
Common name: dogbane

A beautiful yet lethal plant, oleanders are native to the Mediterranean region. They are characterized by their rose-like petals (often a rose pink, though you'll also find white and yellow) and their toxic properties. Oleanders are so poisonous that they'll give you a rash if you touch them, and they will likely make you very ill or kill you if you eat them. As you might expect, this quality has lent itself to quite a bit of lore. The ancient Greeks associated oleanders with the myth of Hero and likely namesake Leander, two lovers who tragically drowned while trying to swim to each other in the Hellespont. In Italy, bringing an oleander into one's home is sure to curse it with sickness or death. And in the Victorian era, oleanders meant "caution" or "beware"—so they're an apt present for your officemate Stevie the next time he tries to steal the packet of M&M's you keep in your desk drawer. (You know, for emergencies.)

Peony

Shame

Family: Paeoniaceae | **Genus:** *Paeonia*
Common name: peony

Peonies are flowering plants native to Europe, Asia, and North America and commonly found in gardens in various parts of the globe. Heralded for their large, showy blossoms, peonies tend to bloom in late spring and early summer and are pretty easy to grow. Peonies carry with them a number of symbolic meanings, including bashfulness and shame, perhaps because of the inward-curling petals that hide their centers. The ancient Greeks even believed that shy nymphs seeking to hide from humans would transform themselves into peonies. Consider wrapping yourself in peony petals the next time you accidentally send a spicy text to your grandma instead of last night's hot date, or bring a peony bouquet to a wedding to give the very drunk best man after his forty-five-minute "toast."

Petunia

Resentment/anger

Family: Solanaceae | **Genus:** *Petunia*
Common names: none

Native to South America, petunias are now common garden flowers in many regions. Their beautiful, multicolored, funnel-shaped flowers make them a favorite among flower enthusiasts; they're also noted summer plants, blooming in early summer through the first frost. Though petunias can withstand hot temperatures, they're also easily damaged, a quality that may have contributed to their symbolic meaning of resentment and anger. Hand out a petunia to the sources of all your grievances, petty or otherwise: the bouncer who wouldn't let your boyfriend into the bar on your birthday, the aunt who spends every family function asking you why you aren't married yet, or the ex who claimed they "just wanted some time to be single," then hard-launched a new partner four months later.

Pine

---◦---

Pity

Family: Pinaceae | **Genus:** *Pinus*
Common name: pine

Pines are evergreen trees native primarily to the Northern Hemisphere and have a significant impact on the ecosystem. They serve as food and habitat sources for a wide range of animals, birds, and insects, and their wood is frequently cut for lumber. Though there are many different genera of pine, pine trees are typically defined by their spiky leaves, fragrance, and soft wood bark. Pine trees have a number of symbolic meanings, including pity, and are excellent gifts for people going through a hard time—like your former romantic partner who just got dumped by your replacement, the neighbors who have been screaming at each other for weeks, or you when you can't seem to unscrew a salsa jar when you *really* want some salsa.

Poet's Narcissus

Egotism

Family: Amaryllidaceae | **Genus:** *Narcissus*
Common names: poet's daffodil, white narcissus

This species of daffodil blooms in mid-spring and distinguishes itself from its parent flower by sprouting white petals instead of yellow; these petals encircle a yellow center disk fringed with red. Poet's narcissus symbolizes egotism, likely because of its namesake, the self-obsessed Greek god of vanity. Your friend who literally cannot stop talking about how hot she is would probably benefit from a few sprigs from time to time—just saying.

Poppy

Eternal sleep / oblivion

Family: Papaveraceae | **Genus:** *Papaver*
Common names: poppy, blind buff

Native to the Northern Hemisphere, poppies are flowering plants known for their brightly colored lobed leaves (the bottoms of which tend to droop as the flower opens), milky sap, and many seeds that scatter in the wind. Those familiar with the classics *The Wizard of Oz* and *Seinfeld* may know that poppies infamously harbor narcotic effects; their seeds contain opium, which is used to make morphine, codeine, and heroine. Likely thanks to their sedative nature, poppies have the symbolic meaning of eternal sleep—just something to consider the next time the neighbor's dog won't stop yapping in the middle of the night.

Rhododendron

―――•―――

Danger

Family: Ericaceae | **Genus:** *Rhododendron*
Common names: rhododendron, big-leaf laurel, bay

Rhododendrons are woody plants native to the north temperate zone, particularly the Himalayas, Southeast Asia, and parts of Oceania. There are many different species of rhododendrons, which are typically large bushes covered with small, colorful bell-shaped flowers. Rhododendron flowers come in a wide array of colors, including pinks, reds, and purples, and can be fragrant or not. Rhododendrons have several symbolic meanings, including "beware" or "danger"; consider gifting a small rhododendron bush to the neighbor who moves into the apartment below your living room, where you will likely be doing loud cardio workouts every morning at 6 a.m. It's not your fault that the gym never has enough clean towels.

Rose
BLACK

———•———

Hatred

Family: Rosaceae | **Genus:** *Rosa*
Common names: none

One of the most celebrated flowers across cultures, roses are perennial shrubs native to Asia, North America, and parts of Europe and Africa, though they tend to be grown all over the world. They're beloved for their beautiful, extravagant flowers, though they're also notable for their thorny stems, which functioned as inspirational fodder for 1980s hair metal bands. Roses are most commonly associated with love (disgusting), but this is incorrect, as some colors harbor darker meanings.

OK, black roses are not *actual* flowers; they do not occur naturally, so if you're handed a black rose, it's probably just a dark red rose dipped in dye. That does not, however, make its symbolic meaning any less withering—black roses symbolize hatred, so if someone does go to the trouble of dribbling ink all over a rose for you, they are declaring themselves your mortal enemy. Return this energy in kind by handing black roses to all your worst nemeses: the sibling your mom loves the most, the coworker who microwaves fish, your middle school frenemy who ruined your life by spoiling the end of *The Sixth Sense*.

Rose
DARK CRIMSON

———◦———

Mourning

Family: Rosaceae | **Genus:** *Rosa*
Common names: none

Dark crimson roses are associated with mourning; they're good flowers to give someone experiencing loss, or keep them for yourself for the next time you wait too long to order a must-have pair of pants and they sell out.

Rose
DRIED WHITE

—————•—————

Death is preferable to loss of virtue

Family: Rosaceae | **Genus:** *Rosa*
Common names: none

Dried white roses have long been given to people in mourning, harboring the symbolic meaning of "death is preferable to loss of virtue." Theoretically, this is to remind those who are grieving that they can withstand loss without losing their values, but it's also an appropriate gift to bestow upon the Tinder match who messaged you, "Your biological clock is ticking," after you forgot to respond to him for a couple of days.

Rose
WITHERED WHITE

———————◦———————

You made no impression

Family: Rosaceae | **Genus:** *Rosa*
Common names: none

A withered white rose offers one of the most devastating burns. Handing one to someone tells them, "You made no impression." Feel free to follow in the Victorians' footsteps and hand withered white roses out to all your rejectees: the date who wouldn't stop talking about Bitcoin, the ex you broke up with before he could break up with you, the colleague who keeps dumping extra work in your lap because she can't be bothered to do it herself. Absolutely not.

Rose
YELLOW

Infidelity

Family: Rosaceae | **Genus:** *Rosa*
Common names: none

Yellow roses symbolize infidelity. According to Arabic legend, the prophet Muhammad once suspected that his wife had been unfaithful. He consulted the archangel Gabriel, who suggested the prophet test his wife's fidelity by telling her to drop whatever she was carrying at the time into the river. If the items retained their color, Gabriel said, she had stayed true to him. When the time came for the test, the prophet's wife was carrying red roses; indeed, they turned yellow in the water. Feel free to throw a few yellow roses at the ex-boyfriend who used to nonstop text with his work wife while you two were hanging out. Yeah, sure, he came home super late from the holiday party because of *traffic*.

Snapdragon

Deception

Family: Plantaginaceae | **Genus:** *Antirrhinum*
Common names: snapdragon, dragon flower, dog flower, toadflax

Snapdragons are cool-season plants native to the Mediterranean region and parts of North America, though you'll find them in many gardens outside those regions. Snapdragons tend to bloom early and come in vibrant shades of yellow, red, pink, orange, and lavender, as well as white. They're notable for their tubular flowers with large mouths that look like closed lips or an animal's snout—when you squeeze a snapdragon's throat, the lips snap open, hence the name. Snapdragons were used to ward off witchcraft in the days of yore and have a number of symbolic meanings, including deception. Leave a small snapdragon bouquet on your partner's side of the bed the next time he swears he vacuumed the whole apartment and didn't just idly run the Dyson up and down the hallway for twenty-five seconds before sitting back down on the couch to play Wordle. Contrary to his insistence, you are not simply manifesting a dust allergy.

Sunflower

False riches

Family: Asteraceae | **Genus:** *Helianthus*
Common name: sunflower

Among the most recognizable flowers on the planet, sunflowers are native to North and South America, though colonizing European explorers brought them back to their native countries in the sixteenth century, and they've since spread widely. They're known for their yellow sunray-like leaves and large disk-shaped centers filled with edible seeds. Humans have cultivated sunflowers for centuries—Dakota, Navajo, Cherokee, and Zuni used their seeds, oil, and flowers for cooking and baking, among other things, and they're still used in food products and as ingredients today.

But sunflowers' beauty and bounty belie a dark symbolic meaning: false riches. Apparently, when Spanish conquistadores showed up in South America to steal the Incas' land, they mistook a field of sunflowers for a massive pile of gold. While this is not an exact metaphor, your boss pretty much did the same thing when she promised you a big raise and gave you an Amazon gift card instead, so feel free to drop a bag of sunflower seeds on her desk in return.

Tansy

Hostile thoughts / I declare war on you

Family: Asteraceae | **Genus:** *Tanacetum*
Common names: common tansy, bitter buttons, cow bitter, golden buttons

This flowering herbaceous plant is native to Europe and Asia and has yellow button like flowers atop super straight stems. In the Middle Ages, tansies were used to treat parasitic illnesses, but in keeping with the era's experimental medical advances, ingesting tansies would often make people even sicker and even kill them. This gave tansies the symbolic meaning of hostile thoughts—in Victorian times, simply handing one to someone could be considered a declaration of war. Just something to keep in mind the next time your roommate "forgets" to take out the garbage . . . again.

Willow

Sadness/mourning

Family: Salicaceae | **Genus:** *Salix*
Common name: weeping willow

Willows are shrubs and trees native to the north temperate regions. They tend to have long, narrow leaves and bark sap that can be cultivated from some species to create salicylic acid, which your dermatologist may or may not have prescribed to you at some point. There are many species of willow within the genus, but perhaps the most well-known is the weeping willow, a hybrid that droops as it grows, giving it a mournful look. This is likely how willows earned the symbolic meaning of sadness; according to Greek mythology, willows were connected with the underworld, and in the Victorian era, they were associated with death and mourning. Hand a willow branch to someone who breaks your heart so hard you grieve: a lover who spurns you, a friend who abandons you, a pet who prefers your neighbor to you . . .

THE

— ◦ —

Maybe
You Shouldn't
Have Given Me
Your Phone
Password

— ◦ —

BOUQUET

Just because you told the ex who cheated on you with a girl he met at the gym that you never wanted to see his two-timing, creatine-guzzling face again doesn't mean you can't give him flowers! The "Maybe You Shouldn't Have Given Me Your Phone Password" bouquet comes with all the right fixings for that special someone who had their own secret special someone on the side. A nice, bright combination of yellow chrysanthemum (slighted love), bird's-foot trefoil (my revenge), basil (hatred), yellow rose (infidelity), and tansy (hostile thoughts / I declare war on you) will do an excellent job of conveying that you hope an air conditioner falls on his head, preferably while the two of them are on a romantic stroll right outside your home. Isn't new love beautiful?

FLOWERS

Yellow chrysanthemum

Bird's-foot trefoil

Basil

Yellow rose

Tansy

1. *Basil*· 2. *Yellow rose*· 3. *Tansy*· 4. *Bird's foot trefoil*· 5. *Yellow chrysanthemum*

THE

—●—

His Mommy Issues
Are Now
Your Problem

—●—

BOUQUET

Breakups are hard, even when the partner you're losing is a psycho-therapist's dream. Then, just when you thought you'd settled into your out-on-the-town single-person groove, BAM—he's got a new girlfriend! Instead of stalking each and every one of her social media pics to document all her most unflattering angles, consider gifting her a "His Mommy Issues Are Now Your Problem" bouquet, a unique blend of withered white rose (you made no impression), pine (pity), and purple delphinium (haughtiness). It's a lovely way to welcome her to her new life of playing girlfriend, mother, therapist, and housekeeper—every girl's wish.

FLOWERS

Withered white rose

Pine

Purple delphinium

THE

—◦—

It's *Not That Hard* to Send a Text

—◦—

BOUQUET

Three months ago, you texted the person you'd been dating for a few weeks to ask if they were down to get dinner on Thursday. You're still waiting for a response, and while your dedication is admirable, at this point it's pretty unlikely that your plans, let alone your future together, are still on. To remind your now-ex that shooting you a quick "Hey, sorry, it's not me, it's you" message might have been better than simply dropping off the face of the planet, assemble an "It's Not That Hard to Send a Text" bouquet. This attractive display includes evening primrose (fickleness/inconsistency), two-toned carnation (parting/no), yellow carnation (disappointment/rejection), and daffodil (unrequited love). Once the bouquet has been delivered, feel free to block this loser's number and make dinner plans with someone else.

FLOWERS

Evening primrose

Two-toned carnation

Yellow carnation

Daffodil

1. *Two-toned carnation;* 2. *Evening primrose;* 3. *Yellow carnation;* 4. *Daffodil*

THE

Just Because
We Parted "Amicably"
Doesn't Mean
I'm Happy about It

BOUQUET

There are lots of different breakups—big blowups, cheating, ghosting—and then there's the slow decline that happens when two people try hard to make it work and ultimately realize they can't. This kind of breakup tends not to be explosive and leaves both parties without a person to be angry with, which is probably a blessing for the friends who have to take sides, but can be frustrating for breakup-ees who'd like to direct their big feelings toward an invigorating anger instead of a seemingly endless sadness. Channel those bad vibes into a "Just Because We Parted 'Amicably' Doesn't Mean I'm Happy about It" bouquet, a stylish mix of yellow carnation (disappointment/rejection), anemone (forsaken), and cyclamen (resignation and goodbye). It's the perfect way to tell your former paramour that even though the split was more or less mutual, you're still unfollowing them on every possible social media platform and wishing them prolonged celibacy.

FLOWERS

Yellow carnation

Anemone

Cyclamen

There are lots of different breakups, and then there's the slow decline.

1. Yellow carnation; 2. Anemone; 3. Cyclamen

THE

—•—

Congratulations
on Dating My Best Friend Instead of Me

—•—

BOUQUET

An unrequited crush is pretty painful. An unrequited crush who picks your bestie over you? Absolutely devastating. Sure, you can't stop people from falling in love with each other, the right one will come for you, yada yada yada, but that doesn't mean it doesn't sting every time you see the two of them making goo-goo eyes at each other at the bar. You could spend the next six months subtly pointing out to your crush how annoying your friend's laugh is, or you could gift them a "Congratulations on Dating My Best Friend Instead of Me" bouquet. Dark crimson rose (mourning) combines with daffodil (unrequited love) and dill (lust) to let your would-be paramour know that you don't like being second-best; once the bouquet's delivered, you can go back to Photoshopping yourself into all their photos.

FLOWERS

Dark crimson rose

Daffodil

Dill

1

2

3

1. Daffodil; 2. Dill; 3. Dark crimson rose

THE

If Your Boyfriend Is Going to Move Himself In, *Maybe He Should Pay Rent*

BOUQUET

After a lengthy Craigslist search, you finally found a roommate to shack up with you in the world's tiniest apartment. Huzzah! Unfortunately, several weeks into living with her, you have discovered she is a demon. In addition to being a slob who refuses to pay rent on time, she also has a boyfriend (fine!) who comes over every single night (less fine!) at 2 a.m. (much less fine! And he always rings the buzzer!), whereupon they fight for two hours before raiding your groceries (HELP!!). Send her a message with the "If Your Boyfriend Is Going to Move Himself In, Maybe He Should Pay Rent" bouquet, an attractive combination of buttercup (immaturity), gladiolus (give me a break), and petunia (resentment/anger). You're probably still stuck with both of them until the lease ends, but this might convince them to chip in for the electric bill. Plus, it looks pretty! Which is good because you're going to watch it slowly die in your own home.

FLOWERS

—◦—

Buttercup

Gladiolus

Petunia

1. Petunia; *2.* Buttercup; *3.* Gladiolus

THE

———◦———

Still Thinking about the $1K I Spent to Be a Bridesmaid at Your Destination Wedding

———◦———

BOUQUET

You were a little surprised when your former high school bestie asked you to be a bridesmaid. Sure, you two were attached at the hip as teens, but she was also the meanest person you've ever met, and the only time she talks to you now is to text you occasionally about how ugly so-and-so got. But you were game to take part in her celebration—why not? Well, many hundreds of dollars, a plane ticket to southern Italy, dozens of bossy emails, and a chartreuse bridesmaid dress later, the "why not?" is pretty clear. You are now swimming in a sea of debt and rage. Instead of writing her and her new hubby a check, celebrate their nuptials by making them a "Still Thinking about the $1K I Spent to Be a Bridesmaid at Your Destination Wedding" bouquet. A blend of black-eyed Susan (justice), bird's-foot trefoil (my revenge), purple delphinium (haughtiness), and orange lily (hatred) will send the message that you do NOT bless this union . . . though you're still down to gossip the next time she wants to talk about your old classmates' bad fillers.

FLOWERS

Black-eyed Susan

Bird's-foot trefoil

Purple delphinium

Orange lily

THE

---

*You Constantly Remind
Me of How Uncool
I Was in Fourth Grade*
but I Can't Break Up
with You Because
We Have History

BOUQUET

Some friendships are meant to last a lifetime. Other friendships are only good for getting the occasional lunch together to reminisce about old times, even though you spent most of those old times getting bullied by your alleged buddy. Sure, you were a nerdy little kid who loved playing fantasy games at recess and never owned the right pair of jeans. But your friend didn't have to tell the whole school that your mom laid out your underwear for you every morning. Anyway, you two are still "friends" in the way that two people become trapped with each other over the course of several decades, but that doesn't mean you're *friends*. Send them a "You Constantly Remind Me of How Uncool I Was in Fourth Grade but I Can't Break Up with You Because We Have History" bouquet, comprising grass (submission), pine (pity), buttercup (immaturity), and amaryllis (pride), and resign yourself to the fact that you two will probably still be hanging out when you're eighty.

FLOWERS

Grass

Pine

Buttercup

Amaryllis

FLORAL ESTRANGEMENTS

1

2

1. Amaryllis; *2.* Grass; *3.* Buttercup; *4.* Pine

THE

---•---

My Favorite Weekend Activity

Is You Bailing on Me Last Minute

---•---

BOUQUET

It's a Friday night, and after a long week of doing business at the business factory, you're ready to let loose with a glass of wine and a cheese platter. You're just about to grab your keys and walk out the door, when you feel that telltale buzz. Your wine-and-cheese-platter pal is "stuck at work, sry!!!!" So much for letting loose.

The thing is, you suspect she's *not* stuck at work; more likely, she just made better plans instead. You suspect this because she did the same thing last week *and* three weeks ago—in fact, this particular meetup was supposed to make up for both of those failed evenings. Now you're likely spending Friday night on your couch rewatching *Scrubs*. You can't believe you put on a bra for this.

When she texts you to reschedule yet again, you *could* set up another hang you know she'll skip out on, *or* you could send her a "My Favorite Weekend Activity Is You Bailing on Me Last Minute" bouquet. A sprightly combination of yellow carnation (disappointment/rejection), purple carnation (capriciousness), and candytuft (indifference), it's the perfect way to tell her you'd rather pluck out your own eyes than waste another night getting ditched.

FLOWERS

—◦—

Yellow carnation

Purple carnation

Candytuft

You'd rather pluck out your own eyes than waste another night getting ditched.

1. Purple carnation. 2. Candytuft. 3. Yellow carnation.

THE

——◦——

I Love It
When You Leave the Dishes in the Sink for Weeks

——◦——

BOUQUET

Not that you're the neatest person on the planet—your desk chair is starting to hold more clothing than your actual closet, after all—but your roommate is a true *slob*. In the eight months you've been living together, you've never seen them clean a toilet or pick up a broom or wear clothes that didn't smell like someone died in them, and you're starting to wonder whether they've ever actually taken a shower. You could follow them around with a vacuum for the rest of your shared lease, or you can let them know it's time to get their act together by giving them an "I Love It When You Leave the Dishes in the Sink for Weeks" bouquet, composed of peony (shame), tansy (hostile thoughts / I declare war on you), gladiolus (give me a break), and monkshood (beware / a deadly foe is near). Note that they'll probably leave the bouquet in the kitchen and expect you to take care of it.

FLOWERS

Peony

Tansy

Gladiolus

Monkshood

1

2

1. Tansy; *2.* Gladiolus; *3.* Monkshood; *4.* Peony

THE

Congratulations
on Dating My Crush Even Though You're My Best Friend

BOUQUET

There's a special kind of betrayal that happens when your bestie steals your crush. It's not quite as bad as a friend dating an ex (or worse, hooking up with them when you're still together), but best friends are supposed to help you get with the object of your affection, not whisk them away with one flirty glance. While you're not *necessarily* going to end a friendship over something like this, you'd be forgiven for spending a month or two plotting out ways to put gum in your pal's hair. Instead, give them a "Congratulations on Dating My Crush Even Though You're My Best Friend" bouquet—hellebore (scandal), mock orange (deceit), petunia (resentment/anger), and marigold (cruelty/grief/jealousy)—then go back to subtweeting them on social media.

FLOWERS

Hellebore

Mock orange

Petunia

Marigold

FLORAL ESTRANGEMENTS

1. Marigold; *2.* Petunia; *3.* Hellebore; *4.* Mock orange

THE

—•—

Every Day, I Hope That Your Life *Falls Apart*

—•—

BOUQUET

There are frenemies—people you compete with and resent but still have some affection for—and then there are *enemies*. An enemy is someone you hate so much, even hearing or reading their name makes your blood pressure spike and your skin crawl. When you see their face, your eyesight darkens; when they're in the same room as you, you can't concentrate because you know the devil is in your presence. An enemy can be anyone: an ex-friend who stole your boyfriend, a former roommate who cheated you out of the rent, a professional contact who tried to tank your career, a stranger who got the last everything bagel at the deli. Doesn't matter—you *despise* this person. Let them know with an "Every Day, I Hope That Your Life Falls Apart" bouquet, composed of basil (hatred), hydrangea (frigidity and heartlessness), oleander (caution/beware), black rose (hatred), and tansy (hostile thoughts / I declare war on you). It's just one shot fired in this battle, but it'll at least let some of the bad feelings out.

FLOWERS

Basil

Hydrangea

Oleander

Black rose

Tansy

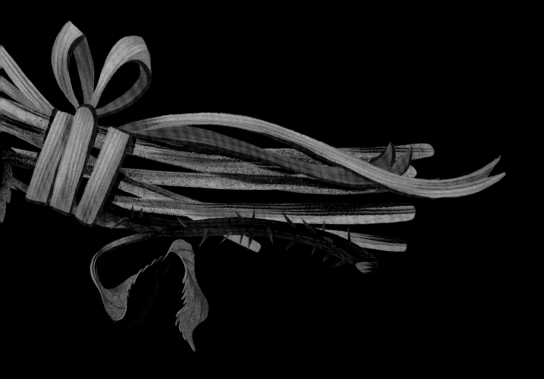

THE

— ∘ —

Congratulations
on Being the
Favorite Child

— ∘ —

BOUQUET

Not every sibling is a dream.

1. Petunia· 2. Poet's narcissus· 3. Yellow hyacinth

There are many wonderful things about having a sibling, chiefly that you always have a playmate growing up, and there's someone else to offer Mom the guest room when she finally loses her driver's license. That said, not every sibling is a dream, and some of them just can't help showing off how much better they are than you at literally everything. Learning to read at six months. Scoring the winning basket at the high school championship. Landing a cushy bank job. Posting on Instagram every thirty seconds so you know *they're* not spending their Saturday night eating Triscuits on their couch and making their Sims fall in love with each other because the outside world is simply too much. They're always making sure you know they're the superior offspring.

Of course, you could field weekly phone calls from your parents asking why you can't be more like Jason, *or* you could give your sibling the "Congratulations on Being the Favorite Child" bouquet, a handsome mix of yellow hyacinth (jealousy), poet's narcissus (egotism), and petunia (resentment/anger). It won't give you their life, but it might make them sneeze a little.

FLOWERS

Yellow hyacinth

Poet's narcissus

Petunia

THE

Listening to Every Movie You Watch, Song You Listen To, *and Argument You Have* Is My Life's Joy

---

BOUQUET

Living in an apartment building has some upsides—for instance, if you're about to get murdered by Ghostface from the *Scream* franchise, there's like a 30 percent chance someone will hear you calling for help—but it also can make you feel a little *too* close to your neighbors. Thanks to the marginal amount of drywall separating you from the folks next door, you're able to hear them do everything all day and night, from vacuuming to talking on the phone to marathoning *The Office* for eight hours straight. Now you know all their family members' names, their preferred workout classes, and that Mary hates when John forgets to unload the dishwasher, and if he REALLY LOVED HER, he would stop playing the video game for TWO GODDAMN MINUTES and put the GODDAMN dishes AWAY. Anyway, let your neighbors know what a delight it is to be so tangentially involved in their lives with a "Listening to Every Movie You Watch, Song You Listen To, and Argument You Have Is My Life's Joy" bouquet. This beautiful display combines black rose (hatred) with orange lily (hatred), basil (hatred), and monkshood (beware / a deadly foe is near), and is a somewhat more acceptable message to send them than banging on your shared wall and screaming, "I WISH YOU WOULD DIE."

FLOWERS

—•—

Black rose

Orange lily

Basil

Monkshood

1. Black rose; *2.* Orange lily; *3.* Monkshood; *4.* Basil

THE

I Love When
You Talk to Me
*in a Passive-
Aggressive Tone*

BOUQUET

There are bosses who offer up tough but fair criticism on your work in the hopes of steering you toward a better performance. And then there are the bosses who prefer to dole out their disapproval in bite-size morsels. There are the "I'll just do this myself" bosses, the "I think we'll have Betsy give the presentation instead" bosses, the bosses who specifically cc'd you on emails to let you know that they did not bring back enough chocolates from their trip to Portugal for everyone in the office, so please don't take any from the kitchen unless they've already told you that you can. These bosses deserve an "I Love When You Talk to Me in a Passive-Aggressive Tone" bouquet, a fragrant combination of amaryllis (pride), hollyhock (ambition), poet's narcissus (egotism), and sunflower (false riches). Hand them one the next time they feign surprise that you got your report done on time, then post your LinkedIn on TikTok.

FLOWERS

Amaryllis

Hollyhock

Poet's narcissus

Sunflower

1. Sunflower; *2.* Hollyhock; *3.* Amaryllis; *4.* Poet's narcissus

THE

Listening to You
Type Loudly
at Your Desk
*Makes Me Want to
Tear My Hair Out*

BOUQUET

Companies claim that open offices encourage inspiration and collaboration, but they are actually torture dens designed in the fifth circle of hell. There are many torments here—the crappy coffee machine, the fluorescent lighting, the fact that you can smell every single one of your coworkers' lunches. But the true demon is your deskmate, who spends eight hours a day making your life as miserable as possible. Whether she's oversharing to you about her sex life, loudly sucking up to your boss when she walks by, or typing with the force of a hailstorm, this person is a living nightmare. Thinking of having to deal with her for a second longer makes you want to quit your job and become a trophy spouse. On second thought, keep your job and give her the "Listening to You Type Loudly at Your Desk Makes Me Want to Tear My Hair Out" bouquet, a combination of tansy (hostile thoughts / I declare war on you), gladiolus (give me a break), and geranium (stupidity and folly). No guarantee that the bouquet will make the noise stop, but it'll at least brighten up your workspace.

FLOWERS

Tansy

Gladiolus

Geranium

THE

You Used to Cover That Medication and *Now I Have to Pay $150 for It*

BOUQUET

Health insurance companies love taking all your money every month in exchange for nothing more than the pleasure of spending several hours on the phone with a representative who lets you know they won't cover a single thing. Sure, the telehealth visit you made to get antibiotics for a UTI was *supposed* to be free, but actually it's $75. The urgent care you went to when you thought you had a flesh-eating disease was *technically* in-network, but since you're on the extra-special (i.e., cheap) medallion aquamarine plan, it cost you $200 to find out you just had poison ivy. And that medication you need to refill monthly that used to cost only $15 is now a "specialty tier drug"—you're on your own, kid!

Instead of sending a death threat through your insurance company's janky claims portal, mail them a "You Used to Cover That Medication and Now I Have to Pay $150 for It" bouquet. This mix of mock orange (deceit), evening primrose (fickleness/inconsistency), and snapdragon (deception) will get your message of outrage across, though it will not make your Explanation of Benefits more decipherable.

FLOWERS

Mock orange

Evening primrose

Snapdragon

FLORAL ESTRANGEMENTS

1

2

3

1. Snapdragon; **2.** *Mock orange;* **3.** *Evening primrose*

THE

—◦—

Thanks

for Peeing in My Bed and Biting the Vet Tech

—◦—

BOUQUET

Pets are an absolute delight. They provide us with emotional support, companionship, snuggles, and ample opportunities for cute viral videos. Of course, the joy of tenderly caring for another life-form doesn't always outweigh all the times your pet acts like a big jerk—whether they're trying to hunt your feet while you sleep or leaving you a smelly "present" inside your new leather mules. The next time your beloved furball terrorizes the Rover so thoroughly that you get a lifetime ban from the app, gift them a "Thanks for Peeing in My Bed and Biting the Vet Tech" bouquet. This enticing mix of daffodil (unrequited love), grass (submission), and candytuft (indifference) will tell your special animal that you will love them forever and ever, even if they rip every single item of clothing in your closet to shreds. And boy, will they.

FLOWERS

Daffodil

Grass

Candytuft

The joy of tenderly caring for another life-form doesn't always outweigh all the times your pet acts like a big jerk.

1. Daffodil; 2. Grass; 3. Candytuft

THE

---•---

Thanks for Calling Me
*during My Sister's
Wedding about
a Report Due in
Two Weeks*

---•---

BOUQUET

Every so often, you get a boss who believes that "work-life balance" means letting an employee occasionally get a few hours of sleep. Your boss has you bailing on after-work plans, answering emails in the middle of the night, and giving up weekends to file her reports. You're having a recurring nightmare that your boss has given you an assignment, the deadline is approaching, and you can't seem to get started. You've had to cancel on your friend three times, and she's starting to hate you for it. And all this—for only a 1 percent annual raise! Give this Miranda Priestly wannabe a "Thanks for Calling Me during My Sister's Wedding about a Report Due in Two Weeks" bouquet, made with poet's narcissus (egotism), begonia (beware), grass (submission), and cyclamen (resignation and goodbye), then change all her passwords and quit without notice.

FLOWERS

Poet's narcissus

Begonia

Grass

Cyclamen

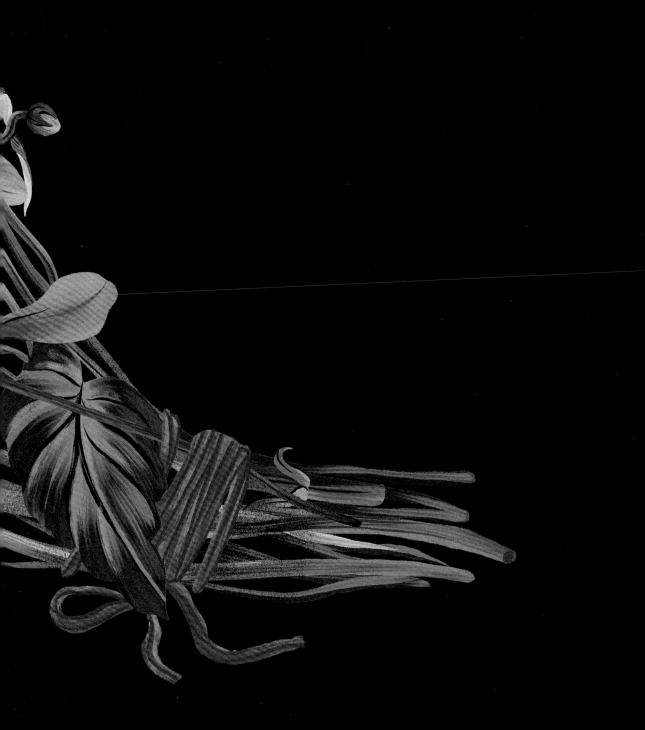

BAD EVERYONE ELSE

THE

My Journey to Self-Discovery *Has Led Me to Discover I Will Never Love Myself*

BOUQUET

All the cheating exes, unappreciative friends, demanding bosses, competitive siblings, and relentlessly barking pets cannot cancel out one simple truth: You are your own worst enemy. Not that you haven't *tried* to embrace all the self-love everyone's always talking about. Yoga? Boring. Meditation? Extra boring. Exercise? Hard. Pop psychology self-help books? Depressing. Practicing gratitude? Thanks, but no thanks. Instead of beating yourself up for being too unlovable even for you, gift yourself a "My Journey to Self-Discovery Has Led Me to Discover I Will Never Love Myself" bouquet, a hefty, fragrant mix of poet's narcissus (egotism), monkshood (beware / a deadly foe is near), peony (shame), willow (sadness/mourning), azalea (fragile love), and amaryllis (pride). It won't remind you that you actually *are* awesome, but . . . you are. Don't let the haters (or the hater bouquets) get you down.

FLOWERS

Poet's narcissus

Monkshood

Peony

Willow

Azalea

Amaryllis

FLORAL ESTRANGEMENTS

1

2

1. Azalea; *2.* Peony; *3.* Monkshood; *4.* Amaryllis; *5.* Poet's narcissus; *6.* Willow

SOURCES

"All about Sunflower: History." National Sunflower Association. https://www.sunflowernsa.com/all-about/history/. Accessed April 21, 2024.

Benzakein, Erin. *Floret Farm's Cut Flower Garden*. San Francisco: Chronicle Books, 2017.

Boekmann, Catherine. "Planting, Growing, and Caring for Columbines." Updated April 15, 2024. Almanac. https://www.almanac.com/plant/columbine. Accessed April 21, 2024.

"Carnation Flower Meaning and Colour Guide." *Bloom & Wild* (blog). https://www.bloomandwild.com/the-symbolism-and-colour-meaning-of-carnations. Accessed April 21, 2024.

Dietz, S. Theresa. *The Complete Language of Flowers: A Definitive and Illustrated History*. New York: Wellfleet Press, 2020.

Encyclopedia Britannica Online, s.v. "azalea," "bird's foot trefoil," "black-eyed susan plant," "carnation," "chrysanthemum," "cyclamen," "daffodil," "dill," "larkspur," "geranium," "gladiolus," "grass," "hellebore," "hollyhock," "hyacinth," "hydrangea," "lily," "marigold," "common monkshood," "common nasturtium," "columbine plant," "oleander," "philadelphus," "peony," "petunia," "pine," "poppy," "primrose plant," "snapdragon," "sunflower-plant," "tansy," "willow." http://www.encyclopediabritannica.com. Accessed April 21, 2024.

Fleming, Kristin, and Michelle Mariorenzi. "Narcissus and Echo." Metamorphoses Project: Tracing Mythology through Time and Place. Cornell College. October 24, 2005. https://www.cornellcollege.edu/classical_studies/cla216-2-a/narcissus-echo/. Accessed April 21, 2024.

Forbes, Maddie. "Cyclamen Flower: Meaning, Symbolism, and Colors." June 25, 2021. Pansy Maiden. https://www.pansymaiden.com/flowers/meaning/cyclamen/. Accessed April 21, 2024.

Gaumond, Andrew. "Chrysanthemum Flower Meaning, Symbolism, and Folklore." Updated March 20, 2024. Petal Republic. https://www.petalrepublic.com/chrysanthemum-meaning/. Accessed April 21, 2024.

Gomes, Janice. "Columbine: A Flower of Meanings." July 25, 2017. Sutro Stewards. https://www.sutrostewards.org/post/2017/07/25/columbine-a-flower-of-meanings. Accessed April 21, 2024.

Greenthal, Sharon. "How to Plant and Grow Candytuft." Updated February 24, 2023. *Better Homes & Gardens*. https://www.bhg.com/gardening/plant-dictionary/perennial/candytuft/. Accessed April 21, 2024.

Hans, Tony. "Carnation Colors: A Guide to Carnation Flower Colors and Their Symbolic Definition." March 30, 2023. GardenFine. https://www.gardenfine.com/carnation-color-meanings/. Accessed April 21, 2024.

Harding, Deborah. "The History of Snapdragons." Garden Guides. September 21, 2017. https://www.gardenguides.com/126335-history-snapdragons.html. Accessed April 21, 2024.

"Larkspur Flower Meanings, Myths, and Symbolism." Updated March 25, 2024. Petal Republic. https://www.petalrepublic.com/larkspur-flower/. Accessed April 21, 2024.

"The Meaning behind the Different Colors of the Carnation Flower." *Happy Bunch* (blog). https://www.happybunch.com.my/blogs/stories/carnation-101-the-carnation-flower-their-meanings-in-different-parts-of-the-world. Accessed April 21, 2024.

"Narcissus poeticus." Gardeners' World. https://www.gardenersworld.com/plants/narcissus-poeticus/. Accessed April 21, 2024.

Roux, Jessica. *Floriography: An Illustrated Guide to the Victorian Language of Flowers*. Kansas City, MO: Andrews McMeel Publishing, 2020.

"Timeless Beauty: Myths and Legends about Roses throughout the Centuries." November 11, 2021. *Amaranté London* (blog). https://www.amarantelondon.com/blogs/blog/the-myths-and-legends-of-roses. Accessed April 21, 2024.